THRIVING
IN THE
THORNS

Restoring Hope & Faith for Women

40-Day Devotional

Brittany Dixon

ISBN: 979-8-9870775-1-1

Book Cover Design: Samuel Rog

Printed in United States of America

To my husband...Forever and always!
To the moon & beyond I'll go...Laila, Caleb and Gabe.
Mom and Dad, thanks for the launch. To my sisters who keep me encouraged.
To **all** of my family, I love <u>each</u> of you.
My mentor who led me to the well.
Friends who I do life with & who support me through & through.

I was in need of a Savior when I strayed far away. God left the ninety-nine to
save (Matthew 18:12-14) the one, like me, in need of rescue.
The gospel of good news redeems, restores and transforms!
I am *never* without hope!

CONTENTS:

Introduction   ii-iii

H.E.A.R Method   1-2

Days 1-10   3-42

Name of God   43-44

Days 11-20   45-84

Name of God   85-86

Days 21-30   87-126

Name of God   127-128

Days 31-40   129-169

Reference   170

About the Author   171-172

This Journal Belongs To

....

———————————— • • • • ————————————

Jesus spent 40 days in the wilderness (Matthew 4:1-11.) He faced difficult trials and temptations. Thereafter, He was launched into His mission and ministry.

Let us emulate our Savior and thrive in spite of the daily burdens and difficulties we face.

We were uniquely crafted and for a purpose! In order to unlock the bigger mission, courageous and obedient faith are necessary to trust God during the cultivation process. *Be encouraged!* God has equipped us with all that we need for our journey.

———————————— • • • • ————————————

"...in Me you may have peace. In the world you have tribulation, but take courage; I have overcome the world."
—John 16:33

INTRODUCTION

Hi friend!

You are seen and loved! Even when God appears absent, His plan works around that which has been lost, taken or mismanaged.

I can imagine us meeting for the first time, and having a conversation over a cup of coffee, or tea if that's your jam. We're sharing laughter, tears, and prayers.

Whether this tough season crosses all areas, or is specific to one, the level of difficulty is stretching your dwindling capacity.

Perhaps, the missed emotional costs of busyness, and the pursuits of "more" have lost glamour.

The struggle of life's detours, and the capability of yielding a hopeful outlook, has nearly run out. The people within the proximity of collateral damage, are unintentionally impacted on account of your empty spiritual cup.

No matter the reason, I want to encourage you that there *is* restoration in Christ! His dividends pay the spirit more, in spite of worldly subtractions.

Recognize the tendency to become embittered with God and your circumstances due to too many divine allowances. Assuredly, in Christ, appearances are *not* reliable indicators of what will come in the future.

This 40-day journal is a venture of the heart through life's thorns, but while wearing new prescriptive lenses.

Let's thrive in spite of the difficult parts of our story. Let's plant seeds of faith, which will soon germinate into peace and joy. What a beautiful hope that awaits those who rest in Christ alone!

Brittany

H.E.A.R BIBLE STUDY METHOD

———— • • • • ————

*G*od's Word supplies our lives with correction, navigation and hope. It's imperative to study God's Word, and to intimately know Him, rather than only knowing *of* Him.

How should we study and apply Biblical truth? This answer varies with each person. The key is to take an introspective assessment into what facilitates understanding and consistency in the application steps.

Above all, pray and ask the Holy Spirit for clarity. Regardless of the Bible study approach, reverence is vital (2 Timothy 2:15.) The Bible doesn't cater to our desires, but rather it requires contextual application. (Galatians 2:20.)

God instructed Joshua to practice discipline in studying the Bible (Joshua 1:8.) This truth, thousands of years later, still applies today.

A relationship with God grows through intentional unhurried time. By studying the Bible, we are provided wisdom and theology that allows for growth, through reverence, in Him.

The Bible may have been physically written by a variety of authors, but the stories are Gods, and He is the inspired author (2 Timothy 3:16.)

Are you ready to H.E.A.R from God? I'm excited for this journey! Let's jump in!

First observe.

Second interpret.

Third apply.

Extract its principles, and then utilize unique application. Scripture is life transformative, and it emerges newness within our hearts (2 Corinthians 5:17.)

God wants to refine us to mirror Christ, even in our suffering. We need pliable hearts to unlock the steps that will follow. The unified goal is faithful obedience to the Holy Spirit. The mindset of the Spirit is to utilize the Word of God to spur on love, not slander. It rebukes in truth, rather than hate. The Spirit praises surrender and humility, while removing any roots of pride.

Steps:
H=Highlight, E=Explain, A=Apply, and R=Respond (Gallaty, 2019b).

Step 1) Each day, after reading the verse, highlight the scripture in the Bible.

Step 2) Explain by observation. Who was this written to? How does it fit in the context of the passage?

Step 3) Application. What does this mean today? What could God be saying, through this, to you?

Step 4) Respond to the scripture. This could be a prayer, or an action to obey.

DAY 1

"Now faith is the certainty of things hoped for, a proof of things not seen."

-Hebrews 11:1

NASB*

The gift of faith allows the intangibility of God to become real. On Him we build our lives. Through faith, we have an anchored hope which sustains us.

Prayer:

Thank you God for this day. You are the Creator of the whole universe. In my trouble, or difficult day, it's hard to comprehend that this circumstance is shaping my story. You are higher than me, and without any limitations. You are a Sovereign God, and spoke the end times while forming the beginning. No person can grasp Your thoughts and expansive wisdom. I seek You for the necessary clarity that only You can provide. Like a child, I'll surrender to Your guidance.

In Jesus' name. Amen.

Gratitude:

Prayer For:

On My Heart:

Praise Reports:

Scripture Rewrite:

REFLECTION

✓ Do I have prior faith experiences to enable my remembrance of God's power?

✓ What is one situation that is stretching my faith?

❖

....

....

....

....

....

....

....

....

....

....

....

Journal Space

H.   **E.**   **A.**   **R.**

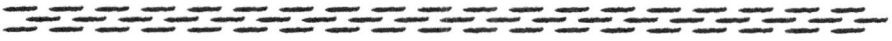

DAY 2

"..and to know Christ's love that surpasses knowledge, so that you may be filled with all the fullness of God."
-Ephesians 3:19
CSB*

A God experience surpasses logic. The measure of love and Christ-likeness expands beyond comprehension. This love pours out to others, and glorifies God.

Prayer:

Dear God, thank you for teaching me that love is unconditional. Striving is not required. Nor must I fill the cavity of my discontentment. My deepest needs, which are in my spirit, are met by You. I need Your daily bread, not intermittent weekly or monthly drop-ins. Your love is so great, and there is nobody like You Lord! I'll build my life on Your unshakeable foundation.

In Jesus' name. Amen.

_____
(Date)

Gratitude:

Prayer For:

On My Heart:

Praise Reports:

Scripture Rewrite:

8

REFLECTION

✓ Define love.

✓ Today, how can I embrace God's love?

＋

....

....

....

....

....

....

....

....

....

....

....

Journal Space

H. **E.** **A.** **R.**

DAY 3

"Consider it a great joy, my brothers and sisters, whenever you experience various trials, because you know that the testing of your faith produces endurance."

-James 1:2-3

CSB*

Trials are undesirable, but they exist for a purpose, and have potential for something greater. Reevaluation of hard times, through a faith lens, reshapes our attitude.

Prayer:

Heavenly Father, the hurdles I face are opportunities disguised as challenges. Around the bend, one day, my character development will repurpose this struggle. Whether a greater battle is up ahead, or if this story is meant to help someone else, I declare Your faithfulness. Although these hurdles are tiresome, I rejoice in the victory in advance. Thank you for revamping the losses and pain points to fashion my better version.

In Jesus' name. Amen.

Gratitude:

On My Heart:

Prayer For:

Praise Reports:

Scripture Rewrite:

— REFLECTION —

✓ How could this trial be serving my spiritual growth?

✓ Refer to Galatians 5:22-23. Which fruit of the Spirit is in the refining fire?

✤

Journal Space

H.　　　E.　　　A.　　　R.

DAY 4

"But Jesus said to him, "If You can?' All things are possible for the one who believes."
-Mark 9:23
NASB*

God has a resolve for every situation. The issue of faith arises and assesses our belief in Christ. Our confidence in Him is predicated by implicit trust.

Prayer:

Lord, teach me the humility necessary to seek Your leadership, rather than my own glory. I want to go wherever You're calling. However, I must first surrender what I think I can control. I'm limited and temporary, but You are an everlasting strong tower. I confess my areas of unbelief. You are an all-powerful God!

In Jesus' name. Amen.

Gratitude:

Prayer For:

On My Heart:

Praise Reports:

Scripture Rewrite:

— REFLECTION —

✓ What underlying heart issue was Jesus highlighting?

✓ Do I trust God's will, even in the ways I am disappointed in His allowances?

✣

....

....

....

....

....

....

....

....

....

....

....

Journal Space

H.   E.   A.   R.

DAY 5

"I am the bread of life," Jesus told them. "No one who comes to me will ever be hungry, and no one who believes in me will ever be thirsty again."
-John 6:35
CSB*

Bread, along with water, in those times, was a staple food in which many solely survived. The analogous statement of Christ is, He's essential. We are invited to experience life in Him now, and in eternity.

Prayer:

Thank you Jesus for Your mercy and sweet kindness. Your grace, considering my offenses, amazes me. I am guilty and confess that I have filled my life with faulty substitute providers that fail. Lord, I'm seated at Your feet, not striving or busying my life with empty distractions. My cup is empty, and I'm ready for God's everlasting sufficiency to daily flood my life.

In Jesus' name. Amen.

Gratitude:

Prayer For:

On My Heart:

Praise Reports:

Scripture Rewrite:

REFLECTION

- ✓ Are there any reliances I cling to? What, or who, are my daily essentials?

- ✓ Am I content as my life is today?

··

··

··

··

··

··

··

··

··

··

··

Journal Space

H.   **E.**   **A.**   **R.**

DAY 6

"For God so loved the world, that He gave His only Son, so that everyone who believes in Him will not perish, but have eternal life."
-John 3:16
CSB*

Nicodemus, an elder within the leadership of the Sanhedrin, had vast religious knowledge. However, he lacked the one necessary thing. Eternal life, with God, hinges on grace through faith in Christ alone.

Prayer:

Thank you God for fulfilling the greatest sacrifice, in order to save me. You made a magnanimous first move by paying the ransom of all on the cross. All You ask for is belief and a willingness to follow. Jesus, I'll follow You! I never want to be without Your love.

In Jesus' name. Amen.

Gratitude:

On My Heart:

Prayer For:

Praise Reports:

Scripture Rewrite:

REFLECTION

✓ Do I believe Jesus is fully God, and Savior? Refer to John 1:1-14.

✓ Am I growing in a Bible-based church? Have I connected with the church body or community of believers?

···

···

···

···

···

···

···

···

···

···

···

···

Journal Space

H.   E.   A.   R.

DAY 7

"Look, I am about to do something new; even now it is coming. Do you not see it? Indeed, I will make a way in the wilderness, rivers in the desert."

-Isaiah 43:19
CSB*

Jesus is the living water for our frailties. In spite of our disobedience, God remains faithful to His promises. In the remnants left, God restores and births new life.

Prayer:

Heavenly Father, I look forward to a newness within You. I'm learning to trust You in every circumstance. Thank you for the rivers You direct into my life. You are my Source, even when hope feels out of reach. In Christ, hopelessness is inexistent because of an anchored hope in a greater end. Even in troubles, You make a way, and meet every need. Your grace grants new life and hope, even though I may experience trouble.

In Jesus' name. Amen.

Gratitude:

Prayer For:

On My Heart:

Praise Reports:

Scripture Rewrite:

REFLECTION

✓ Do I believe God is in control of my life?

✓ Is there an area in need of God's restoration?

❖

....
....
....
....
....
....
....
....
....
....
....

Journal Space

H.   E.   A.   R.

DAY 8

"Rejoice in the Lord always; again I will say, rejoice!"
-Philippians 4:4
CSB*

Having a planted faith and connectedness with God, in spite of circumstances, yields a lifestyle of worship. Our hope in Jesus fills our thoughts, words and actions.

Prayer:

Dear God, I rejoice in spite of present struggles. I'm grateful for spiritual rest, in the midst of any situational unrest. Each day, like a child, I'm learning contentment. My consistent connectedness to You, before the storm, transitions me in and out of grief. My praise and peace will confuse the enemy. Satan will be tired of me when this trial is complete. Lord, thank you for weather-proofing my hope.

In Jesus' name. Amen.

_____

Gratitude:

On My Heart:

Prayer For:

Praise Reports:

Scripture Rewrite:

REFLECTION

✓ Today, I choose gratitude! What are three things I'm thankful for?

✓ Spend two minutes of silence meditating on God's goodness and love.

✛

....

....

....

....

....

....

....

....

....

....

....

Journal Space

H.   **E.**   **A.**   **R.**

DAY 9

"Trust in the Lord with all your heart, and do not rely on your own understanding; in all your ways know him, and he will make your paths straight."

-Proverbs 3:5-6

CSB*

Trusting in God's plan, may not equate to understanding it. Surrender is the strategy that necessitates our prosperity. Our knowledge is second, at best, to His wisdom. He doesn't require our limited counsel.

Prayer:

Dear God, help me to trust Your vast glory in all circumstances. I surrender my fears and uncertainties. I acknowledge and confess my proclivity of self-reliance. Following You, is safer than dependence on my limited perspective. I trust You with every part of my life, even when it seems as if You overlook fixing everything.

In Jesus' name. Amen.

Gratitude:

Prayer For:

On My Heart:

Praise Reports:

Scripture Rewrite:

REFLECTION

✓ Does it feel reckless to surrender to God?

✓ Which area is most difficult to trust God? (All does count.)

———————————— ✤ ————————————

....

....

....

....

....

....

....

....

....

....

....

Journal Space

H.   E.   A.   R.

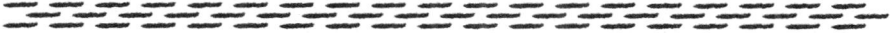

DAY 10

"Say to those with anxious heart "Take courage, fear not. Behold, your God will come with vengeance; the retribution of God will come, but He will save you."
-Isaiah 35:4
NASB*

For anyone battling crippling worry and self-doubt, freedom is available! The enemy promotes fear, but God strengthens us. Christ overcame the world (John 16:33), so we fight *from* victory.

Prayer:

Heavenly Father, I know you care for me. I know that You're aware of the heaviness within my heart. You're concerned about my heart burdens, and when my life is spinning out of control. The anxieties of this season are beginning to suffocate my peace. I desperately need Your help, and to offload my daily burdens! Surround me with Your presence.

In Jesus' name. Amen.

Gratitude:

Prayer For:

On My Heart:

Praise Reports:

Scripture Rewrite:

REFLECTION

✓ What anxieties have consumed me?

✓ Do I have unhurried daily time with God? If not, how can I create this? If yes, how am I guarding it?

....

....

....

....

....

....

....

....

....

....

....

Journal Space

H.　　**E.**　　**A.**　　**R.**

NAME OF GOD

YAHWEH=LORD

. . . .

"And God said to Moses, "I AM WHO I AM"; and He said, "This is what you shall say to the sons of Israel: 'I AM has sent me to you.'"-Exodus 3:14

I remember a time when I flew on an airplane with a visible thunderstorm below the aircraft. It's an unforgettable experience to witness illuminating flashes within the sky, while being spared the crushing sounds and effects of the storm.

Although we weren't in the storm, the staff still prepared us all on the plane for the possibility of it shifting. A change in its course would've impacted the flight.

"Fasten your seatbelts," was announced by the captain. Per standard protocol, even though the flight was uneventful, preparedness was key.

Nevertheless, there are times the storm can't be averted, and a mere possibility becomes reality. A phone call, or just leaving the home into uncertainties of the day, can change the journey at a moments notice.

Moses, in Exodus 3 had a life-altering experience when he encountered Yahweh, the Lord God. First, God revealed Himself. Then, explained His knowingness of Moses. If that wasn't glorious enough, He also foretold the mission buried within the challenges Moses would experience up ahead. That must have been a lot to process!

Whether it's a "go through" or "passing over" season, our sufficient grace (2 Corinthians 12:9) for each day of this journey is from Yahweh, "I Am." We can courageously face the daily unknown, because of our help in Yahweh as our refuge and strength (Psalm 9:9.)

DAY 11

Jesus gracefully disclaims what's entailed ahead. We can ascertain trouble is lurking, but find courage to not lose heart. His promises are the antidote to any hopelessness and fear.

Prayer:

Thank you God for Your divine comfort. You're my daily hope and encouragement. I know You created me for a purpose. I yield to Your leadership, and stand on Your unshakeable foundation. You are an incredible God! Your promise isn't the avoidance of trouble, but in my sustainability within. You've already provided a way out, so all I must do is surrender and rely in You.

In Jesus' name. Amen.

_____
(Date)

Gratitude:

Prayer For:

On My Heart:

Praise Reports:

Scripture Rewrite:

REFLECTION

✓ During hard times, do I attempt to fix the problem or numb myself to it?

✓ Emotions, like car indicator lights, signal the need for reassessment. Do I struggle with controlling my emotions?

Journal Space

H.　　E.　　A.　　R.

DAY 12

"Haven't I commanded you: be strong and courageous? Do not be afraid or discouraged, for the Lord your God is with you wherever you go."

-Joshua 1:9
CSB*

God desires for us to live with boldness, and operate through faith. The solution to any fear is trust in the Almighty. We are courageous, and will overcome whether in the pit or mountain-top.

Prayer:

God, the plan that You have for my life is so amazing! I may not see it, but I trust that it's underway. Your plans are too big for our minds to comprehend. Holy Spirit, flood me with the wisdom needed for the day. In times when You're silent, help me to stay on the right course, and not become discouraged. This is a test of my bravery, and in spite of my fears, I will overcome. I am courageous because of my faithful and all-powerful Protector.

In Jesus' name. Amen.

Gratitude:

On My Heart:

Prayer For:

Praise Reports:

Scripture Rewrite:

REFLECTION

✓ Does this season require bold, courageous faith? In what way?

✓ Which is most difficult for your faith: Bravery for the first step, or endurance in the long middle?

Journal Space

H.　　E.　　A.　　R.

DAY 13

"And He said to His disciples, "For this reason I tell you, do not worry about your life, as to what you are to eat; nor for your body, as to what you are to wear."
-Luke 12:22

CSB*

Peace parallels with trust. Each day, decide to reject anxiety (2 Corinthians 10:4-5), remain prayerful, and rest in Jesus Christ. Worry is needless, and our doubt discredits His power.

Prayer:

Dear Father, You are a marvelous provider. You're worthy of all praises. The fears that used to control me no longer have power, because I'm grounded in You. Your storehouses are never empty, so I trust my daily needs with You. If there's any lack or insufficiencies, I'll remain prayerful for revelation and clarity. Rather than worrying, I'll rest in my hope that You're a Good Father. You care about me.

In Jesus' name. Amen.

Gratitude:

Prayer For:

On My Heart:

Praise Reports:

Scripture Rewrite:

REFLECTION

✓ Do I regularly check my heart for subtle idols?

✓ What makes me the most happy?

Journal Space

H.   E.   A.   R.

DAY 14

"I sought the Lord, and he answered me and rescued me from all my fears. Those who look to him are radiant with joy; their faces will never be ashamed."
-Psalm 34:4-5
CSB*

Believing God's promises in the middle of the storm is made possible with courage. Whistle rejoices while waiting "well." Our unspoken glow is His brilliance in us.

Prayer:

God, thank you for an invite to the table. You're the standard I govern my life and decisions by. I'm resolved, You're the only solution to everything I need. When You allow hard waves to crash, help me to trust rather than doubt What other options have worked? None! Every short cut, and *"brilliant"* self-made solution have fallen short. Lord, You are my only option! I'll faithfully follow You.

In Jesus' name. Amen.

Gratitude:

Prayer For:

On My Heart:

Praise Reports:

Scripture Rewrite:

REFLECTION

✓ Are my reliances in God or my self-made strategies?

✓ Refer to Psalm 34, does my life radiate Christ in my home, friendships, at work, and all that I do?

✣

....

....

....

....

....

....

....

....

....

....

....

Journal Space

H.   **E.**   **A.**   **R.**

DAY 15

*"When my anxious thoughts multiply within me,
Your comfort delights my soul."*

-Psalm 94:19
NASB*

The Bible should regularly scrutinize our thought life. Fears, doubts, and perfectionism are some detriments of over-thinking. Rather, be filled with the Spirit of God and His Word.

Prayer:

Lord Jesus, my mind is clouded with so many thoughts! Unnecessary worry is filling my heart. I am burdened. Help me to grow in worship rather than fear. There is victory available to experience in spite of these troubling circumstances. You subdue my raging emotions, like when You calmed the storm for the disciples (Luke 8:22-25.) My soul is at rest in Your presence. You're the **only** solution to my spiritual weariness.

In Jesus' name. Amen.

Gratitude:

On My Heart:

Prayer For:

Praise Reports:

Scripture Rewrite:

REFLECTION

✓ Do I struggle with any amount of anxiety?

✓ Compare and contrast my coping skills. What's one healthy habit versus unhealthy habit?

❖

....

....

....

....

....

....

....

....

....

....

....

Journal Space

H. **E.** **A.** **R.**

DAY 16

"For I am convinced that neither death, nor life, nor angels, nor principalities, nor things present, nor things to come, nor powers, nor height, nor depth, nor any other created thing will be able to separate us from the love of God that is in Christ Jesus our Lord."
-**Romans 8:38-39**
NASB*

When life threatens our root system, remember that Christ's display of love, and sacrifice sealed unification with those resting in Him. We can't barricade ourselves from the brilliant presence of God.

Prayer:

Lord, forgive me for entertaining the lies of the enemy, rather than holding onto Your truth. Any attack that Satan plans must first pass through Your protective hands. God, of the entire universe, I am hidden from all danger at Your feet , and behind Your arm I'm safe from any storm. Fear becomes obsolete, because I trust You. Whether I live or die, I am victorous in You.

In Jesus' name. Amen.

Gratitude:

On My Heart:

Prayer For:

Praise Reports:

Scripture Rewrite:

REFLECTION

✓ Do I daily expose myself to the healing light and power of Christ?

✓ Am I convinced that nothing can separate me from God? *If* not, journal what feels too divisive.

❖

....

....

....

....

....

....

....

....

....

....

....

Journal Space

(H.)　　(E.)　　(A.)　　(R.)

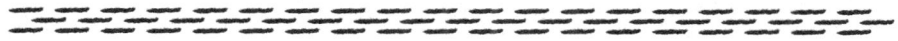

DAY 17

"For he will be like a tree planted by the water that extends its roots by a stream, and does not fear when the heat comes; but its leaves will be green, and it will not be anxious in a year of drought, nor cease to yield fruit."
-Jeremiah 17:8

NASB*

Our lives thrive when anchored into an eternal source. When we are firmly planted in Christ, we endure all seasons, whether it's flooding or drought.

Prayer:

Heavenly Father, thank you for planting me in Your life-sustaining foundation. You nourish my heart's soil and the Word fertilizes all of me. I'm grateful for the remedy of each season of dryness and decay. You equip my heart's foundation to withstand any shift or adjustment in the environmental elements. I thrive in You Almighty God.

In Jesus' name. Amen.

Gratitude:

Prayer For:

On My Heart:

Praise Reports:

Scripture Rewrite:

REFLECTION

✓ Are my peace and joy flourishing in spite of difficult circumstances?

✓ What spiritual season am I in: Winter, Spring, Summer or Fall?

....

....

....

....

....

....

....

....

....

....

....

Journal Space

H.   **E.**   **A.**   **R.**

DAY 18

----- •••• -----

"But seek first the kingdom of God and his righteousness, and all these things will be provided for you."

-Matthew 6:33
CSB*

There is no shame in living with distinction (Romans 1:16-17). Our pursuit is to mirror Christ's righteousness. Therefore, let's stay in the race by picking up and dragging our crosses through the finish line of faith.

Prayer:

Lord, I confess that I've prioritized my plans. I'm sorry for my misplaced trust and self-inflation. Thank you for overflowing mercy in spite of my faithlessness. I'll live solely for You, an audience of one. Christ-like humility and surrender are the foundation of my goals, and my new priority is faithful obedience. My life is not my own, but You living through me.

In Jesus' name. Amen.

Gratitude:

On My Heart:

Prayer For:

Praise Reports:

Scripture Rewrite:

— REFLECTION —

- In order to realign God as number one, what is the Holy Spirit revealing for me to dethrone?

- Take time today, and each day, to confess and recommit my motivations to the Lord.

....

....

....

....

....

....

....

....

....

....

Journal Space

H.   **E.**   **A.**   **R.**

DAY 19

"Do not be anxious about anything, but in everything by prayer and pleading with thanksgiving let your requests be made known to God. And the peace of God, which surpasses all comprehension, will guard your hearts and minds in Christ Jesus."
-Philippians 4:6-7
NASB*

Inner calmness defines a faithful believer who implicitly trusts God. The turmoils of life are weighty, but the empowerment of God secures incomprehensible peace.

Prayer:

Heavenly Father, You're omnipotent, omnipresent and omniscient. You are a righteous Creator and Good Father. There is no problem that perplexes Your understanding? When I'm connected with You, I'm protected against my fears. Your feet fill the earth, and You exist from eternity to eternity. My anxiety is swallowed within Your presence. Thank you for lasting peace in exchange for fruitless anxiety.

In Jesus' name. Amen.

_____
(Date)

Gratitude:

Prayer For:

On My Heart:

Praise Reports:

Scripture Rewrite:

78

REFLECTION

✓ In this season, do I relate more with peace or anxiety?

✓ What have been some hinderances to experiencing peace?

❖

....

....

....

....

....

....

....

....

....

....

....

Journal Space

H.   **E.**   **A.**   **R.**

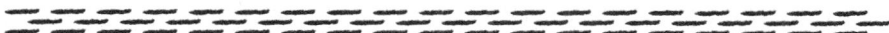

DAY 20

"Come to Me, all who are weary and burdened, and I will give you rest. Take My yoke upon you and learn from Me, for I am gentle and humble in heart, and you will find rest for your souls. For My yoke is comfortable, and My burden is light."
-Matthew 11:28-30
NASB*

The hamster wheel of achievement for the "good" life is exhausting. Spinning our wheels, in search of admiration and value only satisfies temporarily. Christ already gave us worth, so we can rest from striving.

Prayer:

Lord, each day is hard, and I'm tired of daily adversities. One more circumstance may cause me to spiral into depression. I'm at the end of my rope and I need rescue. I know that nothing is impossible for You, but this difficulty is overtaking me. I'm desperate for a soul respite that only You can provide. Thank You Jesus for being my safe place.

In Jesus' name. Amen.

Gratitude:

Prayer For:

On My Heart:

Praise Reports:

Scripture Rewrite:

REFLECTION

✓ Jesus said "come." Have I conceded to His invitation, or am I carrying my own burdens?

✓ What is spiritual rest? Is it achievable when life's busy?

Journal Space

(H.)   (E.)   (A.)   (R.)

NAME OF GOD

JEHOVAH SHALOM=
THE LORD IS PEACE

.....

"Then Gideon built an altar there to the Lord and named it, The Lord is Peace. To this day it is still in Ophrah of the Abiezrites." -Judges 6:24

H ow do we experience peace? Is it achieved when we complete the written goals, that are surrounding it, on our vision board?

It's the golden ticket we bargain and barter our time and resources for. In order to experience peace, we secure residence in safe neighborhoods, save millions in retirement, eat kale chips, climb career ladders, and do more yoga. But, does this work? It's subtly disappointing when it remains out of reach in spite of the one more glass of wine, amongst great friends, while eating a favorite meal, on our dream vacation.

Is peace acquired in the absence of chaos or difficulty? In Judges 6:22-23, Gideon was fearful that death was inevitable after an encounter with the angel of the Lord; this should've been an automatic death. However, Gideon's narrative had a divine *"but"*. For His glory and purposes, God was preparing Gideon for a war victory (Judges 6:14-16) in order to save the Israelites from Midian (Judges 6-7.)

Gideon was told to embody peace, rather than fear (Judges 6:23) because of God's presence with Him in the battle. He and his army were few in number, but impenetrable by divine provisions and protection.

We all have seasons filled with joys and challenges. When God is our foundation, the ups and downs of life can't remove our peace, but rather guard our hearts and guide us through.

In Galatians 5:22-23, peace is one of the gifts of the Spirit. It begins as a seed, but when we live surrendered, it thrives amongst the thorns.

DAY 21

"The Lord is my shepherd; I have what I need. He lets me lie down in green pastures; he leads me beside quiet waters. He renews my life; he leads me along the right paths for his name's sake."

-Psalm 23:1-3
CSB*

> Our soul needs a safe place to snuggle. At God's throne, sitting expectantly at His feet, provides us with our deepest longings and restoration. Even when we stray, we have a trusted Guide.

Prayer:

Lord, You are so amazing, and beyond comprehension. You're the Creator, Sustainer and Protector. In the many pits that I've needed rescue, I was never out of Your sight, and You provided for all of my needs. I don't know what tomorrow holds, but You do! I'm humbled to Your matchless glory. Thank you for the invitation to rest in You.

In Jesus' name. Amen.

Gratitude:

Prayer For:

On My Heart:

Praise Reports:

Scripture Rewrite:

REFLECTION

- ✓ Begin today day remembering that I have all that I need (Psalm 106.)

- ✓ Do I identify with being my own shepherd or God's sheep?

✤

....

....

....

....

....

....

....

....

....

....

....

Journal Space

H.   E.   A.   R.

DAY 22

"Peace I leave with you. My peace I give to you. I do not give to you as the world gives. Don't let your heart be troubled or fearful."

-John 14:27

CSB*

Jesus offers Himself, as the everlasting source of permanent peace. This reliable gift abounds in each circumstance, and never runs out.

Prayer:

Thank you Jesus for experiential peace in any circumstance . In Christ, nothing can threaten my joy, and I'll thrive in times of lack. My peace abounds in spite of the environmental climate surrounding me. I'm dependent on God's wisdom to guide me. If this trial is illuminating issues within my heart, I'll praise You for bringing them to the surface. The better version of myself is being cultivated in every trial.

In Jesus' name. Amen.

Gratitude:

Prayer For:

On My Heart:

Praise Reports:

Scripture Rewrite:

REFLECTION

✓ What are three things that energize me, and fill my cup?

✓ Do I have daily unhurried time with God?

❖

Journal Space

H.   **E.**   **A.**   **R.**

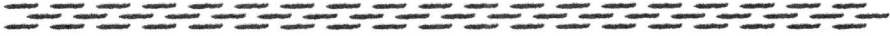

DAY 23

"May the Lord of peace himself give you peace always in every way. The Lord be with all of you."
-2 Thessalonians 3:16
CSB*

The pursuit of peace is on high demand, yet it's rare to find. Be on alert for the counterfeits of peace. It's only when God overtakes our heart and mind, that peace rules in our lives.

Prayer:

Dear Heavenly Father, the Author of peace, I praise Your name. I am grateful for unlimited access to Your throne. You've invited me to experience victorious peace. You fill my life, and for this reason, even when I'm surrounded by trouble, I stand firm in faith. If there is any glory, fame, or honor given to me, I humbly surrender it all to You. It's Yours alone to hold.

In Jesus' name. Amen.

Gratitude:

On My Heart:

Prayer For:

Praise Reports:

Scripture Rewrite:

REFLECTION

✓ Is peace is possible in unchanged circumstances?

✓ Today, I'll remember that the Lord of peace (Psalm 29:11) resides within me.

❖

....

....

....

....

....

....

....

....

....

....

Journal Space

H.   E.   A.   R.

DAY 24

"Guard your heart above all else, for it is the source of life."

-Proverbs 4:23
CSB*

The more cluttered our hearts are with the values and ways of the world, there's less ability to liken after the Spirit of God. The more we fill our hearts with God, the less the world fits.

Prayer:

Jesus, in You I have the ability to discern what should be allowed into my life. Holy Spirit, prune away the things that are not bearing fruit, and God glorifying. If there is any new thing that You are calling me to, please grant the necessary clarity and wisdom. I want to align my life with Your righteous pursuits. My motivation is to emulate Your holiness above all else.

In Jesus' name. Amen.

Gratitude:

On My Heart:

Prayer For:

Praise Reports:

Scripture Rewrite:

REFLECTION

✓ Are there things that are polluting my heart? (i.e. music or other habits).

✓ How does my heart discern the voice of God?

❖

Journal Space

H.   E.   A.   R.

DAY 25

"Cast your burden upon the Lord and He will sustain you; He will never allow the righteous to be shaken."
-Psalm 55:22
NASB*

We have a loving Heavenly Father who sustains us in every situation. God is concerned about us. We can live out peace and rejoice, even if we are in troubling situations.

Prayer:

Dear Lord, whether I'm in high or low times, I'm thankful for You. You are a faithful burden lifter. I thrive within the midst of troubling circumstances. On the other side of this trial, during the good times, I'll remain humble and remember Your mercy. Though the storms will come, its allowance has boundaries that You oversee, and You don't let it completely destroy me. Thank you for holding back more than my eyes are allowed to see.

In Jesus' name. Amen.

Gratitude:

Prayer For:

On My Heart:

Praise Reports:

Scripture Rewrite:

REFLECTION

✓ Who are the "righteous"? Does this define me?

✓ Consider my life disappointments and trauma. Is Psalm 55 difficult to believe?

Journal Space

H.   E.   A.   R.

DAY 26

"Even though I walk through the valley of the shadow of death, I fear no evil, for You are with me; Your rod and Your staff, they comfort me."
-Psalm 23:4
NASB*

We have a loving Heavenly Father who sustains us in every situation. God is concerned about every part of our lives. We can rejoice, even if we are in troubling times. He is watchful and providing for our needs.

Prayer:

Heavenly Father, I feel trapped and unable to go one more day under the weight of my circumstance. I know the origin of my help, so I'm pleading for You to save me from this pit, and protect me while I'm in it. This valley is too deep and wide for me to navigate on my own. Nothing else has satisfied my soul needs. Lord, please throw me Your safety net.

In Jesus' name. Amen.

Gratitude:

On My Heart:

Prayer For:

Praise Reports:

Scripture Rewrite:

REFLECTION

✓ What does the writer of Psalm 23 mean by "the "shadow of death"?

✓ When life seems to cave in, how well do I manage my emotions?

❖

....

....

....

....

....

....

....

....

....

....

....

Journal Space

H.   E.   A.   R.

DAY 27

"...having cast all your anxiety on Him, because He cares about you. Be of sober spirit, be on the alert. Your adversary, the devil, prowls around like a roaring lion, seeking someone to devour."
-1 Peter 5:7-8
NASB*

Our life assurance is in a Heavenly Father who cares. We ought to humble ourselves, and rest in God's powerful hand.

Prayer:

Lord, You are my strong tower. Strengthen my faith, so I can withstand Satan's devised attacks. Nothing will ever separate me from Your love. Goodness and mercy are available in spite of these circumstances. My answer is always "yes" to You, no matter the personal costs. Help me stay connected to You through every inconvenient detour and valley.

In Jesus' name. Amen.

Gratitude:

Prayer For:

On My Heart:

Praise Reports:

Scripture Rewrite:

REFLECTION

✓ Do I have any war strategies when I'm under attack

✓ Are there any areas of sin that the Holy Spirit is convicting me to confess and repent (turn away from)?

Journal Space

H.   E.   A.   R.

DAY 28

"Search me, God, and know my heart; test me and know my concerns."

-Psalm 139:23
CSB*

We should regularly self-examine our hearts and repent of any level of sin. Properly handling our sins, which are God offenses, prevents self-deception.

Prayer:

My God, You know the inmost parts of me. My nakedness is not offensive to You. You created me within the darkness of my mother's womb, and love me unconditionally. I try to avoid Your all-encompassing glare, but You see me as I am. My past doesn't disqualify me, and Your grace paid for my second chance. God's love molds my hardened heart.

In Jesus' name. Amen.

Gratitude:

Prayer For:

On My Heart:

Praise Reports:

Scripture Rewrite:

REFLECTION

✓ Do I question God's goodness because of prior negative experiences?

✓ Have I ever experienced God's unconditional love?

❖

Journal Space

H.   E.   A.   R.

DAY 29

"And which of you by worrying can add a single day to his life's span?"
-Matthew 6:27
NASB*

Yahweh is our provider, so worry is unnecessary. A stethoscope assesses the physical heart, but the litmus for wellness of our spiritual heart health is resilient trust in God.

Prayer:

Lord, I'm not capable of leading my life without Your grace and love. I used to fear surrender, but now I see You're behind the scenes of my life. You've providentially repurposed my failures, and used all parts of my storyline. If any challenge has been allowed on my path, I know there is a greater purpose. Your pen is writing my story. May it all be for Your glory.

In Jesus' name. Amen.

Gratitude:

Prayer For:

On My Heart:

Praise Reports:

Scripture Rewrite:

REFLECTION

✓ Do I struggle with worry? If so, in what area (s)?

✓ Has worry affected my emotional and physical health?

··

··

··

··

··

··

··

··

··

··

··

Journal Space

H.   **E.**   **A.**   **R.**

DAY 30

"The righteous cry out, and the Lord hears and rescues them from all their troubles."

-Psalm 34:17
NASB*

Our storms record first-hand experiences on our resume with God. His deliverance may not be circumstantial relief, but His help is promised. He comforts us in suffering, and provides while we wait.

Prayer:

Father, You hear and see me in the depths of my pit. I know that Your love and goodness screen the allowed battles. Remembrance of Jesus's sufferings balms any sprouting root of bitterness, and extinguishes doubt within my heart. His power provides the necessary bridge over my weakness. Thank you God for the ability to wail and rejoice, without compromise, of Your love. In advance, thank you for my missional rescue.

In Jesus' name. Amen.

Gratitude:

On My Heart:

Prayer For:

Praise Reports:

Scripture Rewrite:

REFLECTION

✓ Is there a current problem that I'm praying for God to rescue me, a loved one, or friend from?

✓ Do I trust God when He solely provides comfort, without a foreseen fix, of the problem?

❖

....

....

....

....

....

....

....

....

....

....

....

Journal Space

H.   **E.**   **A.**   **R.**

NAME OF GOD

YAHWEH-ROHI=
THE LORD OUR SHEPHERD

"The Lord is my shepherd, I will not be in need.." -Psalm 23:1

I shall not want, plays in my head, as I hum the Maverick City song to encourage myself in the busyness of the day. My patience is stretched as my to-do list grows, while the capacity to execute it lessens. The thought popped in my head, "24 hours within a day is not enough!"

Why did King David, in Psalm 23:1, assert such an unrealistic statement? It doesn't seem accurate because I do want, and many things! My prayer needs are constant, for myself and others.

With a long list of wants stretching over a mile long, it's difficult to comprehend the joy and peace heard within this declaration of satisfaction.

Perhaps, King David, found a work around plan, or he's discovered a greater contentment and provision in spite of desires.

Can someone achieve peace when facing the shadow of death (Psalm 23:4)? Yes! The sole, beyond human reasoning, solution in every circumstance, is *Yahweh-Rohi*. His Sovereignty covers every need.

Our past and present circumstances may not be favorable, but God promises to meet the needs of our soul. He, as our Shepherd, knows the plan He has each of us, and how to fill the gaps we struggle with daily.

Have you trusted in God as your Shepherd? His faithfulness fuels our hope when our faith has exhausted. His goodness lavishes our unmet needs, and heals our brokenness. In Him, we do have all that we *need*.

DAY 31

"Now may the God of hope fill you with all joy and peace in believing, so that you will abound in hope by the power of the Holy Spirit."

-Romans 15:13
NASB*

Our hope is fixed in Jesus. He is coming soon. Train the eyes to look onwards to the finish line with expectancy and joyous celebration.

Prayer:

Lord and Heavenly Father, You are my cup filler. The burdens of life drain me, but Your deposits fill me to the point of overflow. I run over into the others lives, and I'll seek how to be a useful blessing. The unconditional love that You've shown satisfies me, and it's all that I need. Regardless of my desires being met or left unanswered, I'm learning contentment (Philippians 4:11-12.) I praise Your mighty name!

In Jesus' name. Amen.

_____

Gratitude:

Prayer For:

On My Heart:

Praise Reports:

Scripture Rewrite:

REFLECTION

- In this moment, does my cup feel empty or full?

- Make a list of five praises I can celebrate in advance, prior to its fruition.

✤

....

....

....

....

....

....

....

....

....

....

....

Journal Space

H.   **E.**   **A.**   **R.**

DAY 32

"For the Lord God is a sun and shield. The Lord grants favor and honor; he does not withhold the good from those who live with integrity."
-Psalm 84:11
CSB*

There is available favor, and Biblical prosperity (not worldly) for those in pursuit of God's righteousness. In Christ, adopted as co-heirs, we have all we need in God alone.

Prayer:

God, You direct my steps. I'll listen to Your instruction, and adhere to Your correction. The Holy Spirit is my navigation. In Christ, I build my life on an unmoving foundation, even with seasonal changes. I pray that I bear much fruit, as a witness to my oneness with You. You are my light and illumination into the dark shadows that are still under construction.

In Jesus' name. Amen.

Gratitude:

On My Heart:

Prayer For:

Praise Reports:

Scripture Rewrite:

― REFLECTION ―

○ Refer to the praises listed in the reflection from Day 31. Does it seem like God is withholding good things?

○ In this psalm, it says "God is a sun and shield", what does this mean to me?

....

....

....

....

....

....

....

....

....

....

Journal Space

H. **E.** **A.** **R.**

DAY 33

"Therefore, prepare your minds for action, keep sober in spirit, set your hope completely on the grace to be brought to you at the revelation of Jesus Christ."
-1 Peter 1:13
NASB*

An anchored hope allows us to flourish, even if a circumstantial win doesn't prevail. Nonetheless, we are equipped & prepared in and out of seasons.

Prayer:

Jesus, You're my unshakeable living hope. If I keep my focus on Jesus, I won't lose my way. If I rely on substitutes as my provider, my self-destruction is certain. The Holy Spirit guides and corrects my footing, and His Word is a lamp on my journey. Christ resets my thoughts, and realigns my hope.

In Jesus' name. Amen.

Gratitude:

Prayer For:

On My Heart:

Praise Reports:

Scripture Rewrite:

REFLECTION

In the verse above, which is the most challenging: preparing, keeping, or setting?

From 1-10 (1=low to 10=high), rank my hope in Christ?

✢

Journal Space

H.   E.   A.   R.

DAY 34

*"I pray that the eyes of your heart may be enlightened,
so that you will know what is the hope of His calling,
what are the riches of the glory of His inheritance in the
saints,"*
-Ephesians 1:18
NASB*

If there is any dark areas in my heart, pray and ask for the Holy Spirit's enlightenment. Our lives change when we're exposed to God's light.

Prayer:

Lord, You have no equal comparison in any way. Help my spirit to remain in awe of Your vast glory, and the richness of Your mercy. Each day, I want to know You more, and how to better follow. All that I will ever need is attached to You.

In Jesus' name. Amen.

Gratitude:

Prayer For:

On My Heart:

Praise Reports:

Scripture Rewrite:

REFLECTION

✓ Some characteristics of God: Just (Psalm 18:30), Eternal (Deuteronomy 33:27), Trustworthy (Malachi 3:6), Unequaled (2 Samuel 7:22), Omnipotent (Jeremiah 32:17), Worthy (Deuteronomy 6:4), Righteous (Romans 3:21-26), Sovereign (Isaiah 6:3).

✓ What is one attribute of God that I want to know better?

⸎

....

....

....

....

....

....

....

....

....

Journal Space

H.   E.   A.   R.

DAY 35

"Set your minds on things above, not on earthly things. For you died, and your life is hidden with Christ in God. When Christ, who is your life, appears, then you also will appear with him in glory."
-Colossians 3:2-4
CSB*

Don't allow old mindsets to impede embracing new life in Christ. We can't prosper by resuscitating dead things, or by living in the shadows of the past.

Prayer:

Heavenly Father, each day I'm reminded to set my mind on Jesus, and to keep it set. I exist to serve and glorify God, the Creator of the earth. Jesus Christ provides the standard to mirror faithful obedience and courageous missional living. My heart is wide open to God, and my will is His. Search my heart for ways that I am living counter to your grace and love, and help me to realign with You.

In Jesus' name. Amen.

Gratitude:

On My Heart:

Prayer For:

Praise Reports:

Scripture Rewrite:

REFLECTION

✓ Write this somewhere to see everyday: "Set my mind on Christ in every circumstance!!"

✓ Think about a recent scenario in which I acted in my flesh vs. spirit. What happened?

❖

....

....

....

....

....

....

....

....

....

....

....

Journal Space

H.   **E.**   **A.**   **R.**

DAY 36

"I am sure of this, that he who started a good work in you will carry it on to completion until the day of Christ Jesus."

-Philippians 1:6
CSB*

Keep going! Until Christ is revealed, our journey is never static. If we are not moving ahead, we slowly, yet assuredly, drift backwards.

Prayer:

Lord, You see my life timeline from beginning to an impending end. You know my capability. My inside out transformation is for Your purpose to shine the light of the gospel. It's in my worst that God sees my best. He is ironing out all of my waywardness for His glory. I am thankful, in advance, for learned resilience and endurance within each trial I pass through.

In Jesus' name. Amen.

Gratitude:

On My Heart:

Prayer For:

Praise Reports:

Scripture Rewrite:

REFLECTION

✓ Do I believe Philippians 1:6?

✓ Has there been a difficult failure that I've tried to move past? Write it out. Using a *red* ink pen, circle and cross it out. Lastly, in *another* color ink pen, overwrite "FORGIVEN."

✦

....

....

....

....

....

....

....

....

....

....

Journal Space

H.   **E.**   **A.**   **R.**

DAY 37

· · · ·

"But as for me, I will wait continually, and will praise You yet more and more."

-Psalm 71:14

CSB*

> Waiting is a verb. Even if physical change may not yet be detected, there is movement within the spiritual realm. Worship anchors our hope to a loving and on-time God, while we wait.

Prayer:

Heavenly Father, by Your grace, I anticipate greatness in my life. I pray for prosperity and favor. It's hard to wait, however I'll wait *well*. I choose praise, each day, rather than complaint. **Gladness,** in one-word, describes my life in spite of the surrounding circumstances that may not align. I have peace in the finality of my story, so I will worship while I wait.

In Jesus' name. Amen.

(Date)

Gratitude:

Prayer For:

On My Heart:

Praise Reports:

Scripture Rewrite:

154

REFLECTION

- ✓ Is there any way I'm waiting on God? How can I wait *well*?

- ✓ Who can you serve, in any capacity, or diligently pray for today?

Journal Space

H.   **E.**   **A.**   **R.**

DAY 38

"Brothers and sisters, I do not consider myself to have taken hold of it. But one thing I do: Forgetting what is behind and reaching forward to what is ahead, I pursue as my goal the prize promised by God's heavenly call in Christ Jesus."
-Philippians 3:13-14

CSB*

What appears to be lost is gain for what's ahead. None of my losses or trials are wasted. The prize at the end is greater than any circumstantial regrets, which are momentary in comparison to eternity.

Prayer:

Thank you Lord, for a life-giving hope in Jesus. I have joy in spite of unanswered prayers. My peace is real, yet if onlooking without a God lens, it doesn't make sense, and goes beyond logical explanation. I realize the burden of my struggles, but the crown of victory, that is soon coming in eternity, is my hope to face each day.

In Jesus' name. Amen.

Gratitude:

On My Heart:

Prayer For:

Praise Reports:

Scripture Rewrite:

REFLECTION

- How do I balance setting goals, yet leaving room for God to make changes?

- Are there any goals that I need to revise, in order to be in alignment with Christ rather than the world?

Journal Space

H.   **E.**   **A.**   **R.**

DAY 39

"And He got up and rebuked the wind and said to the sea,
"Hush, be still." And the wind died down and it became
perfectly calm. And He said to them, "Why are you afraid?
Do you still have no faith?"
-Mark 4:39-40
NASB

Faith requires reliance in God, rather than our feelings, experience, or logic. In Christ, we are holy "sea-walking" one faith step at a time.

Prayer:

Thank you Jesus for Your power. There's no numbing substitute that compares to the longevity of peace that flows from Your throne. In the storm, I'll trust You, even in the middle, when its impossible to find my own way out. Your grace is sufficient, and I can courageously follow You into unknown territories. Lord, help me be brave for You.

In Jesus' name. Amen.

Gratitude:

On My Heart:

Prayer For:

Praise Reports:

Scripture Rewrite:

REFLECTION

✓ Answer the same question that Jesus asked the disciples, "Why are you so afraid"?

✓ Can I remember a time when God built a faith experience from a prior faith triumph. Refer to Habakkuk 2:4.

———————— ✤ ————————

....
....
....
....
....
....
....
....
....
....
....

Journal Space

H.   **E.**   **A.**   **R.**

DAY 40

"You will keep the mind that is dependent on you in perfect peace, for it is trusting in you. Trust in the Lord forever, because in the Lord, the Lord himself, is an everlasting rock!"
-Isaiah 26:3-4

CSB*

> Peace opposes anxiety. God-reliance counteracts self-reliance. Our guarantee to thrive, in any situation, hinges on our foundational core support.

Prayer:

Heavenly Father, I am so thankful for Your promises, peace, guidance, and caring for all of my needs. Even in my worst pits, I have hope! I'm safe in Your midst. Thank you for revealing the new things that You're doing within my life. You've softened my heart, and restored my hope. The thorns in my life won't obstruct my ability to thrive, or experience victory. You are my refuge, and the rock that I'll remain anchored to.

In Jesus' name. Amen.

Gratitude:

Prayer For:

On My Heart:

Praise Reports:

Scripture Rewrite:

REFLECTION

✓ After this 40-day journey, what are two of my takeaways? Where might God be launching me?

✦

....
....
....
....
....
....
....
....
....
....

Journal Space

H.   **E.**   **A.**   **R.**

THRIVE
Courage
Shine

····

"The report of your obedience has reached everyone. Therefore I rejoice over you, but I want you to be wise about what is good, and yet innocent about what is evil. The God of peace will soon crush Satan under your feet. The grace of our Lord Jesus be with you."
-Romans 16:19-20
CSB*

REFERENCE:

(1) Gallaty, R. (2019b, September 23). What is a HEAR Journal: Full
Explanation from Replicate Ministries. Replicate.
https://replicate.org/what-is-a-hear-journal/

ABOUT THE AUTHOR:
Brittany Dixon

Brittany has loved to write for a lifetime, and has authored enough personal journals to fill a library. As her first publicized work, she desired it to be a resource and inspiration for women to get connected to God, and grow in His Word. Regardless of life's season and the spiritual climate within, our hope is unveiled and available in Jesus Christ.

She and her husband live in the Dallas-Fort Worth area, along with their three children. Whether serving in her home, or at the bedside as a Masters-trained nurse, her passion is to inspire women to cultivate an *"all-out-ness"* for Christ.

Courageous Radiance

In 2015, Brittany began to blog, which later expanded to include a podcast. The vision is for a revival within the hearts of women. Spiritual radiance will magnify in spite of life's circumstances, due to an anchor in Jesus Christ.
Courageous Radiance is on a mission to equip, encourage and share practical tools for women to courageously pursue God.

GET ANCHORED.

GET EQUIPPED.

BE ENCOURAGED.

www.courageousradiance.com

Social media:
IG-@courageousradiance
Facebook Group: Courageously Radiant Women

SCAN ME

Made in the USA
Coppell, TX
04 January 2023